Skinning the Bull

John Daniel

Oversteps Books

First published in 2012 by   Oversteps Books Ltd
6 Halwell House
South Pool
Nr Kingsbridge
Devon
TQ7 2RX
UK

www.overstepsbooks.com

Printed in Great Britain by imprint digital, Devon

to Jane again

Acknowledgements:

I should like to thank the editors and judges of the following
magazines/competitions who have previously published
some of these poems: 14, 7th Quarry, Borderlines, dreamcatcher,
Fire, The Interpreter's House, Iota, Moor Poets, National
Poetry Competition, Other Poetry, Oxford Magazine, Oxford
bus posters, Poetry and Audience, Scintilla, Smiths Knoll,
Staple, Tears in the Fence, The Rialto, The Jersey Eisteddfod,
The Journal, The SHOp, The North, The South.

Contents

Success

It was the 2nd Rayners Lane Cub Pack.
I was an Otter.
They were in sets like stamps
the red set
the blue set
the yellow set
shining like jewels in the dust
outside the Cub hut.
I wanted them all.

I set about gardening, first-aiding
and dusting under the bed.
My mother signed a certificate
swearing I had dusted under the bed.
I grew lettuces, applied tourniquets
and swam with my clothes on.
My father signed a certificate
swearing I had swum with my clothes on.
At last I had all of them.
Akela gave a speech to the Pack
as we stood in a ring in the dust.

There are More Important Things in Life
than Badges, he said.
Badges are not that Important.

I left the Otters and joined the Jackals.
I walked past the Cub hut
and hid in the bike shed
where rubies shone in the dark
like mudguard reflectors
and an inner tube slid along in the dust,
hissing, *Success, Success, Success.*

First job

My father shook my hand.
Good luck son!
A man's world, work.

Plates dropped down an aluminium chute,
grease thick as candle-fat,
a kitchen-cauldron stink on everything.

Stalled next to Tom, small and skinny-armed,
a merchant-seaman for twenty years,
arms red as lobsters.

Tureens and food slid non-stop from above.
Don't waste your life like this! I said,
Go back to sea! Do anything!

At five they handed me my cards.
In the Underground I swayed as from a gibbet,
head bowed in filial shame.

Paperchains

That Christmas, sliding white envelopes
into their pigeonholes, I fell in love
with the beautiful next-to-me sorter,
marching forth with my fat sack
of presents, delivering split-open parcels
from a furniture van, naked turkeys
with plump, feathered thighs just in time
for the desperate housewives. We met
in the canteen, clasping hot mugs
in our palms, stamping the slush
from our boots. Then it was over
and I went back to my family, the desolate
dining-room under the paperchains,
bound like Andromeda to the rock of my Christmas.

My mother's kitchen

My mother's kitchen is empty now,
cleared of dead geraniums – the cooker
she could no longer use –
the green cupboards fitted in the 1950s –
the china with the leaping stag –
the potatoes bubbling round the joint –
the recipes on faded paper.

She's wheeled up to the table now
remembering sometimes in a slide of mind
that saucepan, those dents –
a tea-towel with heraldic arms –
the castles she visited in Spain.

Lavender pretties

My mother lives at the end of the road
behind sliding glass doors.
Do you live here? she asks
as I push her past the lavender bushes.
No, I say, *You do.*
Where do you live? she asks
Round the corner, I say
Do you take many people out? she asks
Just you I say.
Oh! she says, *I don't know around here.*
I always pick her lavender which she sniffs.
We used to plait them when I was a girl, she says,
We called them lavender pretties.
Do you live here? she says again
as the sliding doors open
No I say, you do.

My mother is a ship

My mother is a ship
adrift on the open sea
off on the dark waters,
holding her head
as the craft bobs up and down
saying *Thank you! thank you!* to everyone,
while I pass around sweets to the others
Nancy smiling as always
Gwen taking her clothes off
Jean telling everyone
how she fought in the Blitz
Doreen clutching the wound in her thigh
my mother rocking inside
the closed harbour of women
who have all been out and about –
kids, work, husbands,
mottled legs through which
babies have passed;
solitary anchors dropped
in the silt of the carpet
where the tv tolls in the corner
a buoy on the tide
lighting the way home.

Bank heist

Today I took my mother
into Barclays Bank
where she has banked since 1952
but nobody knows her
because they keep changing themselves
like counterfeit notes.
She is probably
their oldest customer
but they are deeply disloyal
caring only about screens and security
and whether she has a driving licence
although she has never driven
and therefore does not exist for Barclays
who suspect us of forgery and false identity
and think perhaps I am Jesse James
pushing his old mother
who will leap up
from under her blanket
and make them all lie on the floor
when all she wants
is for someone to recognise her
because she has been here since the 1950s
like the old coinage.

Sweets

I always bought you
Mackintosh's Quality Street
shining like Cinderellas
in glittering scarlet and purple

sharing them among
the gnarled fingers
twisted like tree-roots
as they lay in their laps.

Today I reach up
to the supermarket shelf
but then I remember
your locked door

and the long corridor
I don't need to go down
again
anymore.

Aquarium at Barcelona

These cinema screens,
moving staircases, the shark overhead
growing its teeth like unwrapping steel,
the sea bass turning and turning
while far below
a moray eel stalks like a tabby cat,
(the Romans used their poison against people).
these luminous gift-wrapped butterflies,
fish in their glad rags, surgeon-fishes
with knives in their tails, warty rock fish with spines,
two hundred times deadlier than cobra, nameless fish
sailing like rocks, mouths open, astonished to be born,
armless fish, flounders with swivelling eyes,
rock-digging mullets, eels on their way to impossible
meadows.

I am connected, my arms endless possibilities,
my sex shrivelling into the flat underside of the ray
coming to land like a spaceship, my gender swivelling,
the doncella's two colours, sequential hermaphrodite,
the deal with clown fish inside the anemone's tentacles,
crawling out of the sea, flippers, fans,
tripods, eyes, lights, stars.
the blotches wink in the darkness as I retrace my steps.
to the mind's black centre
where no halogen light falls, the core in the depths
where phosphor breaks yellow and red,
fishes rising up to the silver tinsel of mermaids,
the twitch of the sole attacked by the ray
the spin-up of sand, the electric spasm of life.

God's doing this, no doubt about it.
Darwin and God, the two of them,
dancing in darkness out of the sea,
up the beach, the brain a squashed matchbox,
the aeroplane shark flying over my head
turning me upside down
to the depths where I'm born.

Darwin

He kept it quiet for 20 years.
and hid the first draft ticking like a bomb
among old racquets, bric-a-brac
and croquet mallets in a downstairs cupboard.

His wife hung pictures of the Scriptures in the hall
to ensure they'd meet again in heaven.

Punch portrayed him as an ape
Oxford thundered.

He stayed at home and grew a long white beard,
held court inside his dining room
as Justice of the Peace, loved all his children,
was kind to servants, took three walks a day
along the sandy path around his garden,
Eden-like, cross-pollinating primroses
or measuring the worms that upheld his whole Creation.

Badger

I use a badger shaving brush
waddling over my face every morning,
hooking the soap-foam, smoothing
my skin. Badgers are suspect
but I suspect those
who suspect them.
I have seen them on infra-red film
cuddling each other, dragging their beds
out in the morning and back in the evening.
The badger is superior
to that cream you squirt out of tubes.
He is plump, moving over the stubble at the edge
of my face. I descend with the blade.
We do this every day, the badger and I
joined in a lather of foam.
Whiskers my father called me
as he came in the door every evening
banging me on the head
with the rolled-up newspaper
before I had any.

Goldfish on Totnes station

19 goldfish wait in a pool
on Totnes station.
They have long skirt-like fins
and glide in a circle of light
surrounded by rocks
and a white picket fence,
trembling with the murmur
of underwater voices
Dundee and Paddington,
Aberdeen, Berwick-on-Tweed
Newton Abbot and Exeter
trains cancelled and late,
journeys delayed and disrupted,
19 bars of soft gold
patiently wobbling in weeds,
exploring the crevices,
a pirate's hoard in the water
where heads come and go
and the sky winks like an eye,
swimming in loops and circles
helping us as we watch them
going nowhere.

Fish

I love you when you watch fish,
giggling at the huge snouty one
that never ventures out of its hole,
other uglies you think could be me,
wrestling with an octopus, oohing and aahing
at silver shoals flying over the reef,
the white and orange fish-clowns
that live among poisonous tentacles,
the sardine-balls chased by the sailfish,
cheering on gudgeon-like creatures
that crawl up the cliff to reach paradise,
laughing uproariously as schools of green tiddlers
surround the grey hippopotamus, hoovering his hide,
nibbling the armoured plates of his arse.

Rats' nest

There was a rat in the compost
staring up as I pulled the tarpaulin
suddenly caught on stage as the curtain went up,
darting back down its tunnel into the black heart.
I felt scared. Was there a nest?
What should I do uncovering the small rat-bodies
like the Princes in the Tower? I should never
have layered the heap with cardboard and newspapers
as advised by the radio.
I dug on cautiously and found a shredded
apartment mercifully empty, abandoned
before the invading spade, taking their young with them,
refugees on the road from the rat-war that never stops,
running for their lives, like millions of others.

Autumn massacre

My neighbour has chopped down
my waterfall of Virginia creeper,
gold, orange, umber, the backdrop
to autumn, covering the 1930s shithouse
built in the corner, the raw concrete wall.
He's a tidiness fanatic. I've met them before,
pruning the world, garden-improvers,
root-choppers. He was clearing the path
nobody walked along. Now it's empty
but still no one walks there, only
the ghost of the creeper, trailing vines
of orange and gold. We need beauty
more than utilitarian battlements
or functional flowerbeds. The stumps
of the roots hold up agonised knuckles
like the Burghers of Calais. I shall erect
a new fence and clothe it with snake-coloured
creepers, mimosa and jasmine.
I shall fight the scourers and minimalists,
the puritan pruners of England.
I shall re-establish the baroque
with bonfires for heretics.
We need to incinerate the incinerators,
we need to return to our senses.

Prague woodpecker

A green woodpecker shines in the jewish
cemetery where I sit quietly waiting
for you among grey, tumbled tombstones
ten layers deep from previous centuries,
a broken ghetto under april trees,
stone generations packed together

as families linked their lives together
treading mosaic pavements where jewish
figurines now stand on mirrors waiting,
while clear above the fallen, unread stones
the woodpecker tap-taps his centuries'
brisk chatterbox against the sunlit trees,

a lively fellow clinging to the trees,
black-capped, yellow mixed with green together
with a splash of red. He could be jewish.
I found your name among the lists waiting
in the synagogue in place of tombstones
for those transported down the centuries

to make the index of our century.
No obelisks for them among the trees
pressed insect-like in lists together.
Kafka saw it walking to his jewish
school – the beetle in his father's house waiting
to escape – the body's stencilled tombstone

breathing , inscribed in every tombstone
of the flesh the crime of centuries.
(The emerald body darts up through the trees.)
Slowly we learn how to live together,
country by country, german, czech, jewish,
christian, muslim, ten lifetimes waiting

for a promised after-life, or waiting
as I do now for you, among these stones
that seek to chart the lives the centuries
have lost, a present love among the trees
that merge their newly-opened leaves together.
Here, in this once-hallowed space of jewish

love and death tourists thread like ghosts
jewish tombstones waiting centuries under trees
for a green bird to stitch our lives together.

Inside and Out

Because you could not come with me
I notice more – red-flamed flowers,
the crested birds with blue-white stripes,
yellow grass between black trunks.

I disappear into the outside
across high walls of black and orange
surmounted by iron spikes,
ranged across the garden dividing leaping grass,

for this is Johannesburg where the gates are locked
and rifles stored in hallway cupboards.
The hillside rocks stand ochre against the skyline
as though they're trying to get in

to this our red-earthed plot where the lawn
is croquet-smooth and a fountain gushes into
goldfish water netted against kingfishers
as we are caged against outsiders.

You fill me still as I stand watching the protea trees
descend the hillside through the yellow grass
to red-spiked railings. An ibis – hadidada – flies over,
There's something sacred here

scratched from the red-brown earth.
Two birds with yellow breasts, black-masked
like tiny gangsters jump in the branches.
We've kept ourselves both in and out.

Africa's not far away, beyond the barbecue
and hammocks, the fountain where the collies drink.
I miss you, balanced between walls and windows,
bars and flowers, prison-spikes and flowering vegetation,

the television screens our hopeful windows
on a world that's more distant than we think.
And love that holds us steady even from a distance
in this wilderness of space.

Eucalyptus

You want me to cut down
the eucalyptus tree in our garden.
It's leaning its steel-grey trunk
towards your bungalow, Osokozy
threatening to obliterate your thin-tiled
roof, your garden with dwarves
wheeling wheelbarrows, the plaster heron
standing beside the netted pool,
sweet peas and dahlias. You accuse
the eucalyptus of planning to crush you
with its down-under weight,
its vast, aboriginal bulk
of desert interiors entering the Osokozy front room,
destroying the cut-glass vases and calendars .
And the leaves, you say in a querulous way,
They fall all year.
Not, I realise, like unselfish English leaves
dropping gently in September, October,
yellows and browns on cold autumn mornings
but thin metal knives, scarlet and silver
not knowing the right season to fall
in their upside-down world, stabbing
gutters and drains, suffocating
the heron-watched-over-pool
where the dwarves trundle their barrows
over the bridge.
I'm sorry, I say, apologising
for the steel-smooth limbs rising above us,
the trunk that sheds its bark like a snake
in ribbons of orange, a grey pillar
holding up the sky in a faraway land
that none of us knows,
I'll do what I can.

Pruning the Magnolia

The magnolia is spreading its arms
across the whole garden, juggling pink
goblets, reaching up to the roof.
It was supposed to be decorous,

a Chinese lady by the lake in pink
slippers. But it has loosed itself
from its moorings, taken ship
with a cargo of blooms, broad-leaved

and brash, colonising the delphiniums
and roses, snuffing out the red-hot pokers,
threatening to take over the garden

with a riotous party. So it has to be
pruned, clipped, curtailed,
trimmed like a poodle with a lavish pink bow.

The Banks of the Nile

Opposite the National Bank of Egypt
(UK Limited) in Waterloo Place,
eating my tuna salad
inside its square cardboard box with transparent lid
not expecting Egypt's National Bank
to jump up like this this after a week of turmoil,
flags, liberation in Cairo's main square,
tanks, 30 years of dictatorship, torture,
the president fleeing, money flowing
perhaps to this very building over the road
at one end of a classical portico with columns, wreaths,
balustrades, as cool as the cucumber sliced
in my cardboard box, arched windows raised in astonishment
leading me to speculate on the intricate threads
connecting those who earn two dollars a day
bundled in cars, blood running down their faces
with this dark-windowed edifice, silent and sphinx-like
squatting on money which trickles like sand
everywhere, even into the tills of Prêt A Manger
advertising *handmade natural ingredients*
avoiding obscure chemicals, additives
and preservatives common to so much food
on the market today as I remember the Nile
overflowing its banks every year
bringing rich harvests as the lights
of the buses shine gold in the rain,
Pall Mall and the clubs where the politicians gather
deciding how to deal with the poor,
the lamps coming on now, the candelabra
inside the bank lighting up underneath yellow shades,
the woman opposite reading The Bible Unearthed
reminding me how we've been through all this before.

Starlings over Slapton

Above Slapton Sands starlings are circling,
rehearsing their tactics, hundreds
whirling in a transparent ellipse, elastic
squeezing in and out over the lake
turning like leaves of a poplar
flickering silver, a shoal of herrings
flecked with October orange,
they bulge and distend, inflate and sink back
picking up stragglers, hitchhikers,
vacuuming the sky, swooping as one,
a clear rubber balloon over the sea,
turning back as if there's an invisible stop.

Perhaps they're in training, strengthening
their wings, learning the tricks of the wind
before they head south. They twist over
the tank that's been pulled from the sea,
its tracks decorated with poppies.
We stand and examine the plaques,
the D-day rehearsals, the tragedy,
while the starlings expand in the light,
a mobile alive in the sky
above the black grief of the tank.

Iron Age fort

We climb to the Iron Age fort
up a path of hazel and hawthorn.

My knowledge of Iron Age forts
is a bit rusty

but I can see this cake-ring
was a high point

in our military history.
War never stops but it grows over,

the bluebells a luminous sheet
covering the long-dead,

the trees a triumphal arch
for the big-eared deer,

staring at us
in the sunlight.

On refusing to buy an armistice day poppy

I'm not buying a poppy this year
I'm not going to remember The Dead

with their blood on my jacket.
I've always bought one before

I've always gone along with the Cenotaph Show
the Laying of Wreaths, the Two Minutes Silence

the Last Post, the Pity of War.
I always thought some were worth fighting for

now I'm disobeying orders
I'm not going Over the Top

I'm not offering to be shot in the head
I'm staying down in my trench

with the rats and the dead
I'm not buying a poppy this year.

Two minutes silence

Two minutes silence to remember war,
a dozen wreaths laid on a stone.
We shouldn't really ask for more.

We've tidied up the mud and gore,
the spattered brains and shattered bone.
Two minutes is enough for war.

We've stood here many times before.
Society allows us to atone.
We shouldn't really ask for more.

Our cause was just, within the law,
Our enemies have reaped what they have sown.
This silence justifies our cause,

Afghanistan, Iraq, Hiroshima.
The minutes soothe us as we stand alone.
We couldn't really ask for more.

The Last Post sounds its sad encore
(Remember to switch off your phone!)
Two minutes silence at the nation's core.
We really shouldn't ask for more.

Music at Blenheim

Queen Anne at one end,
marmoreally dead
white as the statue of a colonial governor

hundreds of leather-tooled volumes
caged behind wire
like red and gold marmosets

when the great chimneyed organ
starts booming Bach
pipes peeling

as we steam downriver
on our paddle-steamer
through savannahs of sound.

Meeting

Where the furrow turns by the oak
they came, two of them, on horseback,
their armour bright as my plough.
Had I seen anyone hereabouts?
Yes, I said, *Ned cutting willow*
down by the river, Hal taking
his black-faced sheep up to the field.
Do you know who we are? the older demanded,
No, I said. The light hit his sword-top.
He fancied himself with his boots and steel gloves.
You fool! the officer said.
His horse backed and twitched.
I've got my barley to sow, I replied,
thick clay and nettles spreading like wildfire.
Rain clouds stacked up behind them,
wintry with long shafts of light.
The younger man slapped the neck of his horse.
We're fighting for freedom and peace, he said,
standing up in his stirrups
and they rode downfield,
kicking up clods in a shower
as I turned back to the plough,
the blade sliding forward
bright as a sword in the mud.

It's simple really

It's complicated. You have to understand
Georgia's breakaway, the arms supplied by the USA,
the trouble Georgia's had with Ossetia,
that pipeline burrowing its way from Ceyhan to the Caspian
Sea – NATO – the intricate labyrinth
of plans and policies
not to mention those flats in Gori
strafed by jets – Stalin's birthplace – you'd think
the Russians would have more respect – but there you are:
bombs, murder, mud. It's simple really:
an old woman lies screaming in a pool of blood.

9.11

1.45 – I'd dropped in The Kite
my Edwardian retreat
sporting prints on the walls –

a woman reading – two boys shooting pool –
a cat curled asleep –
the telly on without any sound

when a toy plane flew on screen
nobody looked as the balls cannoned around
their island of green,

forming patterns and angles
5 hours away
from a cloudless blue american day.

The seven seas

The seaweed lies slumped
on the beach:
cat o' nine tails dumped
from ships that have sailed away
with their captains, capstans and cannon,
canvas, compasses, cockroaches,
over the seven seas.

87,000 coffees

Starbucks does 87,000 drink combinations
all made from responsibly grown
ethically traded ingredients, but they found it tricky
coping with the line of shambling customers
out for the day, eyes rolling, tugging at sleeves,
shouting at strangers, unable to choose between
cappuccino, tall, grande, venti, latte, espresso
and *caramel macchiato.*
One – tall, handsome – couldn't manage words
at all but stood there while his carer
held out her purse for him to practice paying.
We stood behind him as he entered the world
of 87,000 coffees and silently cheered
as he finally got it: *One coffee please.*

Attendant

Canaletto's my favourite.
Not many stop on their way to the Cubists,
36 seconds a picture, the management tells us.
When my eyes start to close I count heads
receding like stars: the Pope, under his panoply,
a pinhead lost in the galaxy,
waves unravelling like knitting,
gondolas black-toothed as the devil,
domes, pillars, churches sparkling like fire.
You can see they're warming up for the evening,
stepping over the boats in their bright satin shoes.
We don't live like that anymore.
I love that one over there, everyone rushing to catch
the lottery ticket, fluttering down from the balcony,
never reaching the ground.

Documentary evidence

I love to think of them
standing on a bench outside the Angel,

Walter Bogan, John Tucker
8 in the evening, Nicholas Gay, William Amyott

a candle on the table, Edward Rounsevall,
shuffling along on the bench

to peer through the broken quarrel
at the Reverend John Prince

holding the thighs of Mary Southcote,
her coats round her waist, standing up

her hands on the wall, Henry Martyn
a diamond-shaped aperture

her hands on his shoulders,
the vicar of Berry Pomeroy, John Prince,

the author of the Worthies of Devon
his back to the wall sitting down

Mary Southcote facing him
standing between his legs

William Amyott, Edward Rounsevall
shuffling along on the bench

to peer through the quarrel
a candle on the table

Mary Southcote, 29
John Prince, 52, holding her thighs

John Tucker, Nicholas Gay taking turns
to peer through the broken quarrel *
her coats round her thighs
her hands on his shoulders

Henry Martyn, John Atherton,
until Nicholas Gay shouts

Fie! For shame on you!
on a bench outside the Angel

in Fore Street Totnes, April 24 1699
about 8 in the evening

*A quarrel is a seventeenth century name
for a diamond-shaped pane of window glass.

Turner at the Tate

When I walk from Turner to the Turner Prize
I walk from seascapes, rolling waves, castles,
pastorals, blazing suns, Dido and Aeneas,
Venice, avalanches in the Alps

into a bare white room with scribbled marks,
a whale-skull concealed behind planks,
gold tracery on the wall, black dumb-bells,
half-images of chairs – tentative, marginal,

and I think *Is this who I am?*
Is this what I feel? Where am I?
and I walk out quickly,
stepping over black girders

back through Gilbert and George sucking cocks
to the Romantics where I feel safe
with the sailors struggling in the water at Trafalgar,
drowning as they go under.

Orchids

The orchids are small porcelain plates
with a spoonful of honey in the middle,

Chinese ladies waving their fans,
beautiful as snakes and climbers from swamps.

Their petals curve back like the fangs of a cobra,
the masks of their pistils are sinister,

carved like the discs on an altar,
miniature gods, in plastic cases

exhibiting their strange, sculptured jewellery
unnatural as art.

'Load every rift with ore'
Keats in a letter to Shelley

I'm not very good at cramming the corners
of phrases, packing the images,
stuffing conceits, passing the parcel of words,
reaching for metaphors up on a shelf,
similes under the stairs.

I'd like to be more like Shelley,
rolling a note in a bottle,
tossing it into the Irish Sea
to bob about in the waves
until someone unrolls it
years later and reads it
just as it was when he wrote it,

salt on the wind, hair blowing free.

Surreal

I left my rucksack in the courtyard of the V and A
while I was in the Surreal Things exhibition
watching the film of an octopus
opening one eye its soft body going in and out
bellow-like its tentacles coiling around
the rocks the attendants eyeing me from a corner
suspicious I was carrying fur grenades
designed to blow us all to a dadaist heaven
when I was only talking to a friend
about French prose and masturbation
in the Fifth Form while they cleared the courtyard
and surrounded my rucksack clinging
to its tessellated pavement breathing heavily
because it was about to explode with
half a century's news fastening its suckers
on a bus map of central London
an inflatable pillow and some dentures
that wouldn't fit.

Farewell to the red pen

My days of red penury are over.
For decades I have wielded it,

a scalpel scattering blood,
delivering subordinate clauses

sprinkling vermillion commas,
it's, its, its' in the margin.

They're, their, there!
The SS hammering on the door of the sentence.

My red dictator hung up at last
like Mussolini (two s's, one n) –

Our non-agreements stretch back
to the beginning. We were never

Compatable, compatible.
I should of known.

Scarlet marks in the snow,
the 40 year crime unresolved,

our bodies criss-crossed in life:
necesary, paralell, seperate.

Story

Sometimes a story comes in.
It usually happens in the morning
when the brain's been asleep
curled up in its fur.
The brain stretches its muscles
and the story comes in at the back door,
throws its coat on the table
like a night-shift worker coming in from work.
It wants to rest
and a story is a kind of rest.
You never know what will happen
as it puts its feet up
and ruffles your hair
while you cook breakfast.

On buying a book of poems by a modern French poet

I treasure the incomprehensibility of language
the impossibility of understanding the old men in the café
talk in the air like fluttering hands,

Ces pages, pistes de décollage
ou de décodage ne suffisent pas.
Les signes me manquent.

I don't want to learn the language of menus
timetables and ski-lifts.
I prefer the puzzle of poems.

Your odd drawings of houses
I half-recognise as my own.
I shall never decipher you fully.

We share the shade like fish
under the leaves in the Lot
seeking the shadows of our small, untranslatable lives.

Prose-poem: a definition

Poetry is in the air. Prose is inside rooms. Prose-poems are in mid-air hovering like helicopters looking for somewhere to land, a rooftop or small pad. Poetry is in the body, prose is in the mind. A prose-poem doesn't know where it is but travels from one to the other and back again. It may be a mule born from Pegasus and a donkey, it picks its way up the rocks of the mountain. It is stubborn for truth, it isn't going to sing but it may dig its hooves in and bray. It can justify itself on both sides. The poem is one-sided and gives itself capital airs, prose is an impossible document covering a million pages. A prose-poem knows its limitations. Poetry is milk, prose is cheese. A prose-poem is on the way to becoming yoghurt. A prose-poem has a story to tell but not a long one. It knows when to shut up.

Lost in Granada

When we're lost in Granada
the girl who serves in the fast-food café
is also a little bit lost,
biting a lip full of rings,
slamming the plates down,
not knowing the way to the Alhambra.

We find it walking the gardens,
the tall, gracious trees,
the cisterns spouting generous water,
the palms floodlit at night
for a drama by Lorca,
the mountains backlit with crimson.

It's what we desire
a fantasy fashioned for tourists
over the blood-stained bricks
of the Moors, the skeleton rooms
of the torturers, the massacres
managed by Christians –

a magic carpet suspended over the city,
gliding over the lights,
the factories, the fast-food café
where the girl sweeps back her hair
and sucks on a cigarette
and plans her escape.

Divorce

We sit in the garden
while your ex re-points the wall.
I planted these you say,

pointing to the jasmine and lilac.
Your son texts you
Don't wake me I wanna sleep

but comes down nevertheless.
We pick our way out
past splintered timbers, bricks, rubble

to your new house
only three streets away
with a view over rooftops,

a cat no one wants,
a man on the internet,
and French windows yawning out

to a lawn with a pond
and two lemon fish
suspended in darkness.

Porn

The important thing
about pornography
is that women
wear shoes and men don't.

If men kept
their shoes on
and women took theirs off
everything would change.

That's why Pan has goat's feet.

Tea ceremony

Today I bought a tea service
from the charity shop,
translucent bone china

lotus leaves and bamboo
I imagine us sitting
cross-legged in white robes

sipping the smoky fumes of lapsang.
We need a change in our lives,
the thick mugs of the sixties

dripping with brown sugar glaze
almost destroyed us
all that spouting of teapots,

saxophone speeches in front of the bookcase
wine spilled on stairs.
We are refining ourselves,

exercising decorum, coming full circle,
accepting the world as it is
gently, without any handles,

cupping the porcelain in the globe
of our palms, enacting our rituals,
balanced, contained.

Buddhist day

I parked across his driveway.
It was difficult for him to squeeze out.
Mea culpa.

It was my buddhist day
My mind was full of the calm sea
rippling softly on to his driveway.

He was a black tempest on the horizon.
He called me an irresponsible git
and summoned a traffic-warden

with eyes blue as the sea.
He was becoming my former self
bristling, ugly,

shouting terrible words,
a waterspout over my calm sea
with the beautiful traffic warden

writing a ticket while my car sat there
pretending it had nothing to do with me.
I thought he would jump on me,

a huge wave against my breakwater
destroying my buddhist serenity
while the traffic warden

with the beautiful eyes
wrote me a ticket,
the new me, the old me,

the three of us
dancing together
on the beach by the stormy sea.

Reading the map

Beyond the edge of the park
and the close-fitting contours,
is the well in the mediaeval forest.
If I look carefully I can see the road
halts at the edge of the river.

There may be a ferry.
There are so many signs to consult,
those cows on the dyke for instance,
the wind twisting the grass,
that beetle jammed between stones.

Someone has been here before me
triangulating my route
fixing me in line with that hilltop,
this school, that house,
providing me benchmarks.

I have grown to love maps,
safe in their plastic cases,
transferring myself to the sheet,
the lines in the grid, numbers,
a sense of the north.

I stare up at the crossroads then back to the symbols
trying to make the two fit,
with me in the middle
and the sun going down –
a winter's evening perhaps –
red between trees.

Here

Here's a house with shutters, balconies
sunlight climbing up and down the steps
where limestone bulges like a giant's pillow
and thin red bricks nestle birdlike
in the hollowed rock.

I need no further panoplies
of glass and steel – mosaic malls,
fountains on a marble plinth,
airport palaces, corporate galleries
strutting in their public spaces.

But here where mortar curls between each stone
widening and thinning as it flows,
design performs continual acts
like swifts that dive in crescent arcs
below the bridge.

It is a place to be. The gods
keep low, working with the years
the jigsaw of the river's loops
the line of poplars upright as distant skittles
the space between the walnut trees

and beneath our feet
smooth-backed pebbles painted by the children
green and purple ladybirds
with dots for eyes and folded wings
out for their evening stroll.

The lodger

Only when he left like a conjuror
tugging endless silk scarves
out of his fist did the contents unfurl.
He must have smuggled everything in by night
or perhaps he made a universe upstairs,
filling the windows, insulating himself from the world.
Of course we knew who he was,
the sound of his banjo escaping
out of the velux window,
always polite when he ventured into the kitchen
to fry ham and eggs, carrying them back to his eyrie
to balance on the edge of an image,
eating off books about string theory
and the emptiness of inter-galactic space.

Button

Today I sewed on a button,
I chose it because it has only two holes,
symmetrical, easy to deal with –
on loan from another gender.
I sewed it on my blue cords
bursting apart, my stomach
pushing against the doors of my trousers.

We don't sew much any more.
You have to pause to sew on a button,
lick thread, eye eyes, finger thimble, hem hems.
The needles lie bright fishbones in black.
We buy clothes made by rows of Chinese
forced to move from their villages,
sleeping in dormitories, not seeing their children.

I make a stalk for the button,
around and around and around with the thread.
It's a bit of a mess from the back. Most things are.
My cords are charity cords – I'm recycling myself,
undermining the Chinese economy.

But I've done it, holding my stomach in,
I've mastered the inertia of life.
I've sewed a button on to my belly –
it's where I began.

Skinning the bull

We haul the carcass up to a beam,
sailors tugging a black sail

that twists round in the barn's gale –
the knife shines in the gloom,

the head is cut off in a cloud of steam
guts flower geranium,

the skin drops in a crumpled heap
a highwayman's cloak

as you kneel and stroke
into the flesh, bone by bone

till the body swings open,
like coming home.

Oversteps Books Ltd

Oversteps has previously published books by the following poets: David Grubb, Giles Goodland, Alex Smith, Will Daunt, Patricia Bishop, Christopher Cook, Jan Farquarson, Charles Hadfield, Mandy Pannett, Doris Hulme, James Cole, Helen Kitson, Bill Headdon, Avril Bruton, Marianne Larsen, Anne Lewis-Smith, Mary Maher, Simon Williams, Genista Lewes, Miriam Darlington, Anne Born, Glen Phillips, Rebecca Gethin, W H Petty, Melanie Penycate, Andrew Nightingale, Caroline Carver, John Stuart, Ann Segrave, Rose Cook, Jenny Hope, Christopher North, Hilary Elfick, Jennie Osborne, Elisabeth Rowe, Anne Stewart, Oz Hardwick, Angela Stoner, Terry Gifford, Michael Swan, Denise Bennett, Maggie Butt, Anthony Watts, Joan McGavin, Robert Stein, Graham High, Ross Cogan, Ann Kelley, A C Clarke, Diane Tang, Susan Taylor, R V Bailey and Alwyn Marriage.

For details of all these books, information about Oversteps and up-to-date news, please look at our website:
www.overstepsbooks.com